Untold Fortunes

Zoe Mitchell

i

Advance Praise for *Untold Fortunes*

"In *Untold Fortunes*, Zoe Mitchell shows us the unflinching magic of women. Whether those women are placed in the modern everyday, the historical or mythical, there is power in every one of their stories. Mitchell never turns away from the difficult or disturbing, while bringing unsung achievements and new perspectives into the light - all of which makes this collection a very rewarding read."

—Kate Garrett, author of
To Feed My Woodland Bones

"With scintillating lyricism and incisive wit, *Untold Fortunes* pivots the ancient European trope of the witch to face itself in a moon mirror. Embracing the mutable light of myth and history, Zoe Mitchell seeks the painful truths behind the eldritch lore, drawing into her lunar orbit unruly women from Medusa to Tonya Harding; WWII engineer Beatrice Shilling to a modern British office-worker. Alive to the realities of political violence, yet disavowing faith in supernatural remedies, these curious, nuanced, metaphysical poems chart their own fearless rise to the challenge of meaning-making in a seemingly indifferent universe. While tenderly grounded in the poet's lived experience of economic precarity, maternal love, friendship and self-sufficiency, Mitchell's feminist poetry plucks on nerves drawn taut across millennia of nihilistic patriarchal power. Skillfully lineated in stanza forms suggestive of terse ballads and medieval infernos, her lucid music will have you believe that 'the moment' is still ours to grasp."

—Dr Naomi Foyle,
Reader in Critical Imaginative Writing, University of Chichester

"Zoe Mitchell's *Untold Fortunes* is part rumination on what the world may promise, and part realisation of what it delivers. In this ethereal, yet deeply grounded poetry collection, the moon's ever-changing roles as supporting character, critic, silent protector, and indifferent lover are observed like a morality play set in the theatre of the self. Despite exploring its share of darkness, the true beauty of this collection is in its core message that while the moon cannot make its own brightness, we each possess the ability within to create our own light. This is poetry that makes you want to run at life full bore. A love letter to individuality and carving out a new path when the one set out for you isn't good enough."

—Dean Rhetoric,
author of *Foundry Songs*

"*Untold Fortunes* unspools in bruise-coloured ribbon around women condemned by the world for summoning the very magic needed to survive it. Through these injustices, Mitchell considers the promise inherent within the title's double meaning—what undreamed lives might exist beyond the ones taken or denied? The poems in *Untold Fortunes* are bathed in cold lunar light and, like life itself, offer no easy answers. Instead, reading them is akin to defiantly pressing two fingers against the beating jugular: *I am still here.*"

—Glenn James Brown,
author of *Ironopolis* and *Mother Naked*

UNTOLD

FORTUNES

ZOE MITCHELL

Mitchell, Zoe / author

Untold Fortunes / Zoe Mitchell

Poems

ISBN: 979-8-9997732-0-3

Library of Congress Control Number: 2025945564

Edited by: Amanda McLeod
Book Design: Amanda McLeod
Cover Art:. Lazarev / tatianazaets via iStock
Cover Design: Amanda McLeod

PUBLISHER
Animal Heart Press
1854 Hendersonville Rd. Ste A
PMB 211
Asheville, NC 28803
www.animalheartpress.net

For My Mum, Pam Mitchell.

"And though she be but little, she is fierce."

Midsummer Night's Dream, Act III, Scene 2

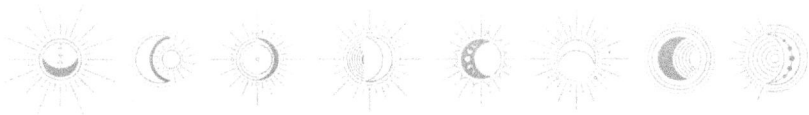

Contents

New Moon

The moon knows a fresh start
may not feel anything
like a revelation or an opportunity.

What arises from the black fabric
is not always an improvement.
You could lose a job and people will talk

about doors closing and opening as if
it's ever that simple. You could gain
an unwanted gift, a new burden.

Change comes from the moment
when all that is altered is something
inside you, something in the dark.

This is just the beginning.
No one can see you, you aren't
really here, there or anywhere yet.

Look up to the sky and seek
the slimmest curve of pale light –
one day, none of this will matter.

Untold Fortunes

Beware of the past, it changes.
Death may be a constant
but the shade of recollection can shift
until all you see are a string of memories
like unpatterned beads -

catching the eye with iridescence
and appearing as different colours
depending on the light.
So very enchanting
until they slip their ribbon
to bob about in dark water.

All of your happy-ever-afters
are two-sided cards.
The world may promise
to sit in the palm of your hand
but it will keep on spinning in darkness.

Accept that the future has you
in an unbreakable contract.
Sign your name and mean it:
the price of any alternative is your life.

Seek the truth in the present,
the now you're breathing in.
A bowl of ice cream is truth.
A niggling ache, a brush of hands,
a fading bruise.
Time unfolds second by second:
this moment is entirely honest.

Forecast

On my first night on earth, there was a halo around the moon.
No one bathed in hospital strip lights could see it;
this was the moment of my arrival, no one was looking out.

This is the moon I was born under; I started screaming in a fever
but what could I have known then? A change in the weather,
a fear of the dark, a sense of becoming my own disruption.

In the grey wash of December, the blanket of night is never quite
thrown off and the winter moon remains, patient and ghostly,
watching the real work of our days as well as our dreams.

She is always there; her milky eye blinks slowly as I fumble
and stumble on cold pebbled beaches and rutted pathways.
She was there when I laughed and sang myself home,

there too on the night when I had to quicken my pace.
There she was, watching and doing nothing.
The moon expands with my secrets, contracts with the days

in a month, the months in a year, the years in a lifetime.
Her indifferent surveillance is constant and holds
an unknown purpose that is neither romance nor

disappointment. I sometimes forget what I was born
knowing – a full fat baby, soothed with pale lunar milk,
blood streaking through my veins like a wild hare.

Divination

We light candles against our fear of the dark,
spill blood, shuffle cards, kiss the crystals,
watch the skies and above all, we dream.

We ask questions the future cannot answer.
Success and failure are all the same there,
neither are the search you're meant for.

We never learn what rests in our question –
the future whispers in our ears but we never listen.
It's right there.

Waxing Crescent

Spend an afternoon in a bar
with a friend, remember everything
you've lost. Press on the bruise

of all your failures, learn
to smile at them because
they are smiling at you.

Feed your heart's furnace,
paint colour on your pale cheeks,
stand at your fullest height.

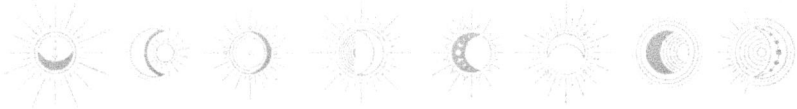

Origin Story

There was a young woman, beautiful
in the way they all are, almost interchangeable
with their gentle, painfully human concerns.

She thought about potential suitors,
her next meal, different ways
to untangle a knot in silken hair.

Before, she hadn't even thought
about the future but she held faith
in its benevolence within her soft skin.

After, she testified that people watched
as she fled from a brawny, gill-necked deity.
She remembers uproarious laughter.

She can't recall what she was wearing,
it's not etched with enough depth for her,
but lawyers will scratch that fact

with acid. The crime is not enough
for the court; she will be burned
by the lines of her dress and flowing hair

as if they matter more than a sanctuary
defiled, or a woman. Athena witnessed
the rape at her altar and had rage enough

to topple a whole council of gods,
but no power to tackle this one,
who held the pull of the tides and took

whatever he wanted. No one spoke of that
when the verdict was given, or how they expected
a mortal to do what a goddess couldn't.

The hand over young Medusa's mouth
wasn't shame – it was the venomous snake
of a story that turns people to stone.

Step

"No one controls my life but me… if there's something in there I don't like, I'm going to change it." Tonya Harding

Don't tell me you hadn't already made your mind up
when I first put my blades onto the ice. When I skate,

your fairy-tale imagination murmurs to your eager eyes
asking for proof and it doesn't take long to find it –

big hair, electric blue eyeliner, a frayed costume and music
blaring so loud you know without listening that like me,

it will be sweating and wicked. If you started earlier in the story,
you'd see what it took to get here, you'd know how thick make-up

hides scars and bruises, broken nails are a sign of hard work
and every missed stitch and sequin comes from a hand shaking

after a long shift. It's not ladylike for you to know anything
so inconvenient and your ethics never extend to anyone

who doesn't look like you. I wasn't plotting anything more
than to hide those flaws, a pristine score to wear like a pelt.

It doesn't matter that I try to hide the join, it will be circled
like a foundation tidemark around my neck. When you see

what you think is a cheap woman grow rich with talent,
you take her for a brazen new bride to a hapless man, an unwanted

ugly step-sister born with a swinging hammer in her hand. Admit it:
you had me cast as a villain long before a princess arrived on the
        scene.

Tut and mutter over the notion of fair play if you must, and tell
　　　　yourself
the gaudy interloper deserved it – a competitor but not a natural,

you'll whisper, then hiss, *not one of us.* I always knew that.
I read the same stories you did and watched the same movies,

the only difference is that I didn't have to wait for your indictment.
I already knew how stubborn this story would be – but so am I.

Heat those iron shoes in a fire brash as a tabloid, strap them
on my feet and I'll dance. That's not spite, honey. It's survival.

First Quarter

There is grace in the night sky. Look up,
make plans, imagine what life
would be like if it were fair.

Now accept that it isn't.
Book the ticket anyway. Even if
you don't have the time or energy, apply.

Write it all down, solemn
as a childhood promise and tick tasks
off the list, one by one. The stars weep

for you so don't slow down
for something as insignificant
as your own tears.

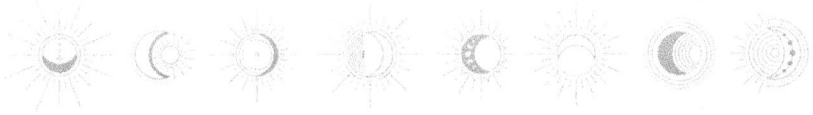

The Vale of Ancient Trees

Persephone stands in the arrival lounge from the underworld:
ancient yews twisted with everything they've ever seen,

lurched into an archway of darkness, a triumph hard as iron
wrapped in poisonous foliage, budded with arils that promise

sudden death among the blooming. Treading with care
through the hushed corridor, she carries the baggage

of another new season, the scent of wildflowers her passport
to the light. She greets the shadows of animals trapped

in tree bark who guard the bare earth, awaiting her return.
The skeletons of dead trees on the steep down remind her

of darker seasons, when the forest writhes around her and stubborn
tree trunks transform into the inevitable red frame

of a departure gate. When the time comes, she will check
her pockets for anything that won't travel – a nursing juniper,

an excess of April showers, carefree laughter – then descend
with chalk dust on her boots, back to the birdless grove once more.

Sensational: The Art of Pixie Colman-Smith

The future sounds green.
Artichokes, brussels sprouts,
parakeets, pears, rosemary,
frogs, leprechauns, tourmaline,
alligators, cucumbers.
Moss. Grass. Trees.

The future feels yellow.
Canaries, bananas,
butter, Big Bird, sulphur,
turmeric, post-it notes, submarines,
pacman, lemons.
Flames. Cards. Sun.

The future smells blue.
Orchids, peacocks,
lagoons, smurfs, robin eggs,
sad songs, Neptune, sapphires,
blueberries, topaz.
Sea. Sky. Eyes.

The future tastes red.
Strawberries, tomatoes,
phone boxes, roses, lipsticks,
apples, stop signs, peppers,
ketchup, fire engines.
Wine. Blood. Hearts.

Waxing Gibbous

Lace up your boots so the cords
are even and tie a bow
that won't come undone.

Eat your evening meal slowly
and don't starve yourself:
you're not that hungry or that alone.

Go for a swim, expose pale
and cratered flesh to the air. Breathe
in time to the water's music.

Immerse yourself in all you loved
before you learned too much.
Trust in the coming, rounded

certainty that all you are has room
to grow. You know where you're going,
don't leave yourself behind.

Periwinkle

When he first gave me periwinkles, blue
like my eyes, I saw an evergreen love,
one that tasted like smoky lavender.
We picked a pair of leaves from the same stem,
cast a spell designed to last forever.

We made a home and planted blue buttons
all along the border. They remind me
of the promise I made, my destiny
served to me on those salver-shaped petals,
those blooms that thrived among the narcissi.

Under the blue bruise of a summer sky,
those petals grew violet like his eyes,
the colour of dusk gathering darkness
when pink light sinks into heaven's palette
and before night locks the door.

Long trailing stems spread across the garden,
choking out all other bulbed or leafy varieties.
I know now that crushed leaf of periwinkle halts
a bloody nose, the crimson of a split lip,
any flow from a woman's body.

Madame Blavatsky, Queen of Cuffs

Behold, we have before us something unremarkable –
a baby girl, not worth educating, born into corsets

and codes of conduct. Now look at our great Madame,
who took that punch in the stomach and never flinched.

The blows kept on coming – a dour look, two bulging eyes,
an excess of chins – but she stayed on her nimble feet.

Next came the gold ring that manacled her to a man
more than twice her age. She tore through those bonds

as if they were paper, unlocked the door to a library
and found so many other worlds in those books –

some you can reach by crossing an ocean if you dare,
but others lie back in the unfathomable past or beyond a veil.

Not content to dream, our Madame woke up and went in search
of new gods from the East, who blessed her freedom.

Watch her now, waving her hands as she speaks of spirits;
light fractures through the rubies and garnets on her rings.

Has she travelled to occult lands, conversed with otherwise
mute apparitions? Ladies and gents, we must try to unravel

the conundrum – does she have power beyond the mortal realm?
This much we know: here was a most unpromising woman,

stout and untidy, and she cast her azure eyes across continents,
lived with lovers, smoked cigarettes and hash with abandon,

wrote books as if no one had ever tried to cinch her in. Perhaps
she had dubious morality, but she gave comfort to soldiers

when they needed it most, cured mothers and beloveds
sick with horror at otherwise irreparable loss.

We can't say it was all hokum when she unwound every rope
that tried to bind her, held her breath in the water tank

of whispered gossip and flat accusation, escaped every time
someone strapped her in a straitjacket.

Rebellion is as the sin of witchcraft and stubbornness is as iniquity and idolatry

My mother taught me how to be a witch.
Her silent craft didn't manifest to me
until it was too late to reject the lessons

and by then I had no wish to unlearn them.
In my last year of school, I was sent home
with a note about my skirt, resting 1.3cm

above my knee. Mum read the rules carefully
then bought the longest skirt she could find
in school colours, even though the hem frayed

and caught under the tread of my DMs.
In the face of the administrator, I saw
the moment my mother's soundless curse hit home.

She mustered in me a mute defiance, a cure
for petty regulation and arbitrary limits
and she did it all without ever saying a word.

Her best tricks always took time to exert their power.
When my older sister studied at that same school,
she didn't own a big coat and one cold day

she wore a denim jacket under her blazer.
Mum knew it was against the rules and wrote
a note explaining that it was all she had

but detention followed anyway.
For years, every time Mum visited the school
for any of her three daughters, she wore

a denim jacket and looked every teacher
square in the eye. I could tell you more –
times when she stood taller than her usual five foot two,

when she wouldn't move an inch, and the full extent
of her long memory. From her I've learned to brew
fermented curses, proven inside the barrel staves

of every time she took a stand or stewed
in a cauldron filled with moments when she wouldn't
let go of doing what was right for her daughters.

There is a poem that I want to write...

... that will be filled with swirling witches
spinning sulphur and cobwebs
around a woman until she breaks their spell.

In this poem, she remembers
her own inimitable power. She smiles once
at the hovering hags at their work

and then, like a cat, shrugs them off.
She will brush dust and ash from her clothes
and walk herself into this poem

that I want to write because my heart
wants to feel that triumph. I want
to walk with this woman into white space.

Full Moon

This is the moment
you've been expecting – or dreading.
Howl if you want to, let it all go.

Keep on screaming. Pick a fight
or fall in love - with yourself,
with someone else, or with all

your many careful choices.
This is a test. Either hide in your house,
pretend it's too cold outside

and you're too busy or
put on a new blue jumper and drink
iced cocktails with no thought

of work in the morning.
The light you live under is tidal;
it rises on the whim of an ocean.

Whether or not you're living
the life you hoped for,
you can't blame the moon.

Blonde Bombshell

Blonde hair, lush curves and sweetly parted lips.
Ogive breasts, clipped boat-tail shoes and hips
like the earth piled in front of trench territory.

She knew that with youth came bankable beauty,
with money came power. She was ensnared
with her eyes open, drank from the chalice

of fame poisoned with barbiturates, the crystal
glass of formaldehyde to fix her as a force of nature.
Detonation became an inevitability;

she wrote the spell that killed her, conjured
out of commodities and consumed like hot dogs,
apple pie and baseball cards. She had been strong

and safe inside the outline of an unreal woman,
but that skin could not age with her. She stepped away
with a tilted walk, a fixed smile and her power.

Miss Shilling's Orifice

The Merlin engine had the war disease, a distinct lack
of magic. It would not allow men to dive or swoop
away from an attack and left them in thrall to g-force
as the flooded carburettor took them far from any hope

of Avalon. Young men in winged armour plummeted
into oceans of fire and water; one brief shining moment
of elemental awe before each Spitfire and Hurricane
was caught by yawning gravity. The pilots learned

too late that there never was a Camelot; wartime women
already knew this truth. One among them shrugged off
the shackle of chivalry and with unrepentant brevity
and a gruff demeanour, wearing oil-smeared overalls,

changed the course of the war. Men laughed
when she arrived at an airbase, but not for very long.
They called her Tilly like the chugging army pick-ups
they drove their troops around in, but never to her face.

Miss Shilling, engineer, found a way to joust with German
fuel injection using a modest brass thimble with a small hole
that became her namesake. A woman who had already tinkered
with her destiny had no problem fixing a simpler engine.

Tool-laden, she braze-welded brass collars to the planes
herself, not caring that she had no place at the officers' table.
Off she would roar on her Norton motorbike, heading
for the next airbase, leaving the pilots in her dust.

Notes on Mistletoe

Mistletoe is an evergreen parasite.
The sticky seeds can burrow deep into the trunk
until a tree is nothing but a prop

with its heart plumbed dry.
This plant can hollow the crown of its host
and yet carries all possible life on a wing.

Some stories suggest it can keep you safe
from enchantment but those tales
are working their own charming illusion.

A man may kiss any woman he pleases under
the smooth-edged leaves and waxy white berries.
Bad luck befalls any woman who refuses.

The juniper bush thrives under mistletoe;
meanwhile, the oak tree dies where it stands.

Making Medea: A Recipe by Belle Gunness, Murderess

Start with a world where men
are in charge of everything,
including a woman's value.

Make that decorative.
Make quiet devotion, gentle
good looks and the ability

to bear children essential –
you need to make more men
to keep this cooking.

If a woman doesn't measure up,
ignore her. If she grows strong
enough to help herself, laugh.

Simmer this situation for years.
If children disappear, don't stir
the pot in case you end up

having to feed them or ask
where they came from.
It's best not to know.

You will find men may also
disappear. Assume coincidence –
you've already decided

that men wouldn't go with
a woman like that.
At the last moment, you will see

she had a recipe of her own:
a bottle of poison, a hacksaw,
a hammer, a pit.

Set a fire and ask yourself
if she died in the blaze
or whether you hope

she withstood the heat
in the kitchen, slipped out
and ascended towards the sun.

Waning Gibbous

The night can sometimes form a blanket
of soft light. Take off those boots,
cancel your plans and rest with a book.

A reading light holds enough warmth,
a ceramic tea pot will pour the perfect cup
every time. There's no need to feel guilty

about any of your pleasures.
The night may bring a ringing phone
that pulls you away until you're sitting

in a hospital waiting room with someone
who isn't sick but does need attention.
Even when you're hollowed out,

you will keep answering those calls.
Back home, the tea is long cold,
but so many pages are waiting.

Spell for a Better Day

The shrill horror of the alarm clock.
The stubbed toe,
the toothpaste stain on your shirt,

the smell of hot coffee breath
from a man standing too close on the train,
the routine delays.

The bruised and already overripe banana,
the bitter taste of a swallowed scream,
the surprise deadlines.

The spot forming on your chin,
the number on the scales,
your split ends, your split family.

The hairline crack of pressure,
the moment you had to smile
through your tears,

the way light fell on your face
to spotlight all your flaws,
the shadow of an angry moon.

Wrap this day into a tight ball,
swallow it with red wine at midnight.
Keep it with all the other days;

each one wrapped in a violet ribbon
embroidered by silver needles in gold thread
with the words 'fuck you, I'm still here'.

Jenny Greenteeth

In a certain light, anyone can see it –
the sickly green of her skin, the film of algae
behind her eyes, the sour olive of her breath,
the leaves of flaked skin at her elbows.

The dull silver of her shadow can stalk you
and like her, it knows children never listen,
that the elderly and frail will always fall.
I must warn you to keep her at arm's length –

she'll push you in the water, laugh
while you're drowning, torture you
for hours if she feels like it, finish you off
with her sharp jade teeth in a single bite.

She scratches, pierces, drowns and devours,
she cackles and dances then she basks
in the water, her hair splayed – a violent neon
frame for her nauseating pea face –

and she's sated for a while. This woman,
this razor-toothed, grudge-infected
river hag who was only ever meant to be
a soggy cautionary tale, she is my sister.

I used to live with her by an emerald riverbed
churning with the possibility of falling
into the water and landing on malachite rocks
slick with moss and her brackish malice.

My only hope is to sever myself from her.
I swim in blue pools with safe straight lines
and chlorinated water, watching for pond scum
and gathering plankton in the corners.

Mrs Duncan Won't Keep Mum

During the Blitz, the air hummed with voices
and women listened.
You might say that what we did back then
was indistinguishable from magic.

Mrs Duncan overstepped when she chose
grand performance halls over drafty huts.

It's nothing against the woman – her sort
weren't brought up like that. A factory girl
may keep her word just as well as any
in the aristocracy, but not her.

A self-made woman would sooner give up
her new fur coat than obey anyone.

The crater of damage she caused claiming
the angels brought her black-edged telegrams
was vast. She pressed on bruised hearts, made them bleed,
charged a fee while releasing state secrets.

That was why they dusted off the old rule,
an ancient label to cover her mouth.

A lenient charge compared to treason
when that would have seen her hanged. We all lost
some liberty in those days, all of us
at work in the shadow of the gallows.

The cardinal rule: when women blab,
men will die. She conjured her own prison.

Last Quarter

Pretend all you want.
Craft a mask of red lips
and winged eyeliner – you know

that what you're doing is bad for you.
Don't waste any more time.
Face a mirror in wavering light,

look yourself in the eye and accept
your own apology. You will wake up
in the morning and go to work,

but for now, the moon knows
that you are sorry
and you are trying your best.

Unforgiven

I keep my past under my pointed hat, it's nothing
to be ashamed of but I don't know,
can't know when the wind might change

and the embers of an angry fire might catch the hem
of my skirt. Time is so unyielding. It's too late
to allow for nuance when the stocks have been set out

in the village square, when a rope hangs ready
from permanent gallows. It's already too late
for too many and only the executioner stands

to gain anything substantial. I used to think it mattered
if you had right on your side, but too many accidents
are condemned, too many lessons left unlearned.

There are too few reasons to change anything now.
Everyone has their tribe, their version of right
and there's no room on any side for a mistake.

I am afraid to live in an age without redemption,
when even sweeping up the ashes from the latest
witch-burning pyre doesn't raise a single question.

We're living in the watchful season when you must
stay concealed when you look out of the window;
glance carefully over your shoulder; pick up every stitch.

Phaeton's Legacy

There is nothing the earth can say;
steaming and hissing from oppressive heat
she leans into the caverns of the dead.

This is what comes from fighting fire with fire –
a scourged soul wrenched from a bruised
body, cooked-ripe, everything scorched

by the same flamed fingers that snatched
every cloud from the sky. She knows better
than to turn her gaze to heaven. The gods

are nothing without thunderbolts and rain.
A mother uses ravenous fire to light her way
as she picks through the ruins. She seeks pieces

of her son – even a stripped bone would at least
give a home to her tears. Ceaseless weeping
from the daughters of the sun does nothing

more than bring them all to the suffocating tomb
of a man who thought he could outrun nature.
Seven sisters meet in despair, grief rips at their hair

and their skin, their nails broken and bloody
from raw scoring on their souls. One tries to fall,
lie still and wait to die but finds herself calcified

upright. Another tries to help but her feet
are rooted into the ground. A powerless, frantic third
looks on and pulls leaves freshly sprouted on her skull,

where her hair had been. Soon their legs are encased
in wood, their pleading upraised arms sway as branches.
Bark circles their waists, their thighs; the rough skin

of the earth's lungs smothers their breasts, their hands
and between their legs. Only their mouths are left free
for splintered cries to their mother, who tries to haul

them out until their grieving screams turn pleading.
The bodies of the sister-trees are one with each trunk;
they tell their mother of the savage, ripping pain

of savage, ripping hands until their voices are felled
by the stiff rind on their new forms. Men mourn
their personal losses, they kindle hate as if

they were alone in losing a son. Or light. Or air.
All of men's yearning is cut down by the earth's
relentless necessity. Grief cedes to the service

a mother demands and men bitterly whip
the sun into rising again, lashing out at the fiery
god and a dry world strewn with bodies.

Such are the spoils of man's ambition.
The earth's hopes are whispered between
women; they weep amber tears, their

sorrow soluble only in oil. Knotted poplar
trees bear witness to the soft wood of sisters,
the promise carried along the bright river.

Paying the Toll

Perhaps I deserve to be locked in here.
I don't understand the clamour of creation
but these thick stone walls make sense to me.

It is not the cold that makes them damp,
it is so many years of women weeping, soaked
into the foundations before rising up

as barriers that muffle the world and keep
the other people out. When a tired prisoner
is bumped up the steep steps towards

a dank cell with a low ceiling, blood
can erupt from a stone. The sharp edges
wear smooth from use but a bruise

contains as much blood as a cut might
and colours itself with a greater grief.
I am never quite alone – politics and nuance

squeeze themselves through the barred windows,
debtors and criminals take their places
on a bare floor as if they belong here.

The walls of this prison are lost on me:
wherever I'm taken, I will keep returning here.
My heart was built for a love I never found –

I can't fly or find a platform to leap from,
chains rust on my limbs, rattle in the wind
and stop me from reaching up, or out.

Robin, Son of Art

Dame Alice Kytler was familiar with power;
a gombeen with the estate of four dead husbands

and an understanding of how to wield magic.
The demon Robin was a sleight of hand
she used to slip her bonds and her country:
mistress of the art of leaving other women to explain
the shadows cast in the scheming darkness of fire.

To follow her example, stoke a blaze of oak-logs
and place the skull of a decapitated thief above it.

Fill the empty vessel with worms,
entrails, dead men's nails, shreds of the cerements
of unbaptised buried boys.
Add a pinch of herbs mixed
in a way you've kept to yourself.

Whisper incantations over the brew
in a hot dark room of hunched women.

The art will emerge in the flicker of candlelight,
pillars made with horrors and wicks
aflame with an acrid hair-burning smell
that brings the demon who loosens
your tongue, your limbs, your every inhibition.

Olga Hunt's Broomstick

I was eighteen, camping with friends
on Dartmoor. Exams behind us, we knew
everything then, thought our vivid certainty
would last forever. We sat around a fire,

poked at poorly baked potatoes, persevered
with cheap sweet wine until it tasted
of our laughter. Night gathered us closer
and we shared stories suited to the shadows,

seeking a reason to clasp a cold hand
and cluster in pairs. One boy told the tale
of the Hound Tor rocks, eyes bright swaggering
as he recounted vicious dogs, tooth by sharp tooth.

Ripping through the fabric of the stories
and darkness, a woman appeared among us;
her wry, wrinkled face displayed fathomless
age, her eyes brimmed with ingenuity and mischief.

She danced with a broomstick bridled
across her shoulders; the husks of the brush
tied on with coarse ribbons of bright colours.
We were as still as the surrounding granite.

She let out a cuckoo laugh and waltzed
into the sinister black beyond the night sky,
brandishing her broom at the moon.
We each went to our separate tents after that.

Now I have a job I'm good at. I wear suits
and earn promotions. Each working day
I am spat out by the hot mouth of the tube
into a cool high-rise beetling with indifference.

On a day like so many before and ahead,
the memory comes back to me full tilt –
the taste of bad wine and first kisses,
intense connections, flames licking at the dark.

Much else has faded but I would still swear
that as she left us, I saw Olga Hunt
take a quick, nimble step over her broomstick
and, quite impossibly, take flight.

Waning Crescent

Before you head back to darkness,
see a movie that makes you laugh
at the horror. Have an early night.

Don't scratch any itches, you will shed
your skin soon but what's underneath
is too tender for this night air.

The moon will know the right moment.
Let sleep curl against your spine
and keep you warm in dreamless sleep.

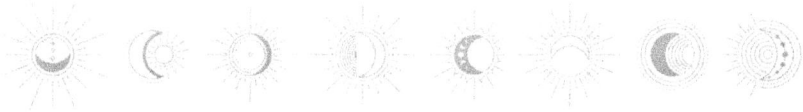

Lies Will Weigh Them Down

"She'll come back as fire / to burn all the liars, / leave a blanket of ash on the ground."
          Frances Farmer Will Have Her Revenge on Seattle – Kurt Cobain

Rapes, rats and other horrors.
Dirt floors and hosepipe baths
to punctuate the days between outrages.

That's what the public wants –
a victim, a martyr, an actress but
never just a woman.

Frances picks the petals
from a primrose flower,
and then sets them all aflame

to render any lies about her
to ash. She haunts the world
as a thorny witch to prick

a liar's conscience. She stays, too,
for those who know her truth
and what it is to face the madness

of sedated and screaming reality
in an antiseptic beige walkway,
the wrong side of a heavy locked door.

Maybe she's born with it

These walls have ears and eyeballs and limbs
and organs embedded in the brickwork.
The bloody countess stained the foundation,
contoured the bailey with buried bodies

and tossed others in locked rooms no one
ever thought or dared to check. Thick stone
muffled the screams and while whispers travelled
further than they should, it wasn't quite far

enough. Elizabeth Bathory gave the masonry
a waterline, walls wept as her dark desire insinuated
overlines into each of the four towers
and smoothed the wrinkles around her iced eyes.

She was chatelaine to chains, hot metal
and sharp implements, queen of the last cut.
She watched in panting fascination while
women were stripped raw, doused in cold water

or honey, left to freeze or be eaten alive.
She bathed in the gore, her face smeared
with human greasepaint, kohl-ringed eyes drawn on
with blackened, charred remains. Her victims'

names were perfume, infusing her with longing.
She bore the fatal slap of vanity until
she was bricked up against a world of reflections
and died alone with her pitiless beauty.

Night Mothers

The race to capture the sun begins
at dusk. Old women wriggle on scabrous
bellies and crawl out from under mountains.

They run or fly frantic in forests, they search
city rooftops and under the foundations
of village homes, they call to each other

as the stars appear, they turn over stones.
Each crone brandishes a brace of vipers,
asps or adders in an attempt to rattle the sun

but darkness always prevails. Defeated by black
silence, they slither into a dry well, leaving
their scaly bouquets behind. The night mothers

are deep underground by daybreak.
Last night they failed but they are patient.
The sun must set. It will try to rise again.

Chanctonbury Ring

I wonder, as I lie peaceful on the rabbit-cropped turf,
looking at the wreckage of implanted trees
that never should have been there,
how anyone could think that a hill was haunted,
inhabited by demons or that it hated anyone.

There are stories of the devil stealing souls here,
of Caesar and his army appearing,
treasure seekers, lost children, a woman in white.
Perhaps this is a place for understanding loss,
the part it plays in our history of gains.

Reports of ghosts and broken nights come from men –
men who are tough, men who know better
or didn't know before then exactly what they were,
how vulnerable in nature, how afraid
of screaming women in the empty dark air.

Away from the city, away from cars and phone signals,
away from the artificial world, something else
finds a voice. I know they're not witches, they're women
in pain, ignored until they find
their roofless home on an ancient hill.

The Bell Witch Makes a Friend of Darkness

I was born among the petty jealousies
of a village overrun by feckless men,
spurned women and bored children.

I became the implicit threat of darkness,
the creeping dread in an unlit hallway,
the absence of any other explanation.

I got out when I could, moved on
to the fertile landscape of ghost stories
in search of something like rebirth.

No devil came and bid me serve;
people did that. I was followed here.
They cast me in a pit. I clawed my way out.

Now I take flight in the night sky,
rest in the dimmest, half-hidden corners
and patiently wait in a sullen cave.

I can slip between shifting clouds,
tramp crisp autumn leaves underfoot,
take form in a beam of moonlight.

These days (and nights) I haunt as I please
and this misty existence leaves me free
because I was never here.

About the Author

These poems were written as part of a PhD in Creative Writing, examining witchcraft and creativity. The poems look at historical and mythical witch figures, and contrast with truly monstrous women. Many of the poems are more personal, using witchcraft and magical metaphors to address my own personal experiences, including the years when I completed my PhD.

I write to make sense of the world, and use my feminist perspective, fascination with mythology and a sharp sense of humour to find a way to frame the world to tilt it towards making sense.

My poems have been published in numerous print and online journals, including *The London Magazine, The Journal of the British Fantasy Society* and *The Rialto.* My first collection, *Hag,* was published by Indigo Dreams Publishers in 2019.